# BETWEEN
# DYING AND BIRTH

## Sermons for the
## Lenten Season

## Robert S. Bachelder

BETWEEN DYING AND BIRTH

0236/ISBN 0-89536-623-1

*For Beverly*

# CONTENTS

# INTRODUCTION

Paul admonished the Christians in Rome: "Do not be conformed to this world, but be transformed by the renewal of your mind . . ." Henry Vaughan, the seventeenth century English poet, gave voice to a kindred sentiment in "Quickness":

> *False life! a foil and no more,*
>    *when*
>      *Wilt thou be gone?*
> *Thou foul deception of all men*
> *That would not have the true*
>    *come on.*

Our lives are usually some combination of the "false" and of the "true," are they not? We mean to be able to say with the Church through time: "*Kuriakos!* We belong to the Lord!" At the same time, however, we know that our ways conform all too closely to the ways of the world, and that the true life has yet to "come on." So it is that in "Ash Wednesday," T. S. Eliot could pen this line: "This is the time of tension between dying and birth."

"Teach us to care and not to care," Eliot continues, and that is the aim of these Lenten sermons. To speak of things which bring life and things which bring death. To suggest how the heavy drapes which enfold the human soul, the Church, and our world may be pulled back to let in the light of God.

The origin of the word "Lent," it is thought, is an old English term derived from the agricultural practices of pre-Christian England. The word is *lencten* and refers to the lengthening days of the inbreaking springtime. May our lives in this Lenten season be graced with ever-lengthening days. Out of the "tension between dying and birth" may we emerge with renewed faith, deepened insight, and a bolder witness.

# Your Money and Your Life

## ASH WEDNESDAY
## Matthew 6:1-6, 16-21

*"But lay up for yourselves treasures in heaven . . ."*
— Matthew 6:20

In his classic treatise on politics, *The Republic,* Plato observed that the greatest enemy of justice is the family. Yes, the family! I daresay his claim will strike you as being rather silly. After all, most everyone agrees the family is a good and necessary institution. Sociologists continue to say the family is the vital unit or cell of society. We are all disturbed by the disintegration of the family as the divorce rate climbs. Many believe this phenomenon is as dangerous as running out of energy or leaving ourselves vulnerable to an enemy attack. This is why "family life" is one of two national priorities of our United Church of Christ. Here we are, then, focusing our efforts on preserving the family, and now I come along and say with Plato that the family is an enemy of justice. I have some explaining to do!

Years ago the Harvard political scientist, Edward Banfield, went to the little town of Montegrano in southern Italy. He wondered why its people could not deal with the problems confronting them. They desperately needed a school and a medical facility, but they could not organize for action. The reason for this, he discovered, was their overwhelming parochialism. Everyone behaved according to the rule: I will act only

maximize the material advantage of my own family.
anfield entitled his study: *The Moral Basis of a Backward Society.* In a backward society, loyalties are too narrowly conceived to create a community.

Geographically speaking, Montegrano may be far away, but spiritually speaking, it is close to home. With our dominant philosophy of "looking out for number one," we are becoming as parochial as the people of that little village. We are on the way to becoming a "backward society."

Let me be specific. A couple of years ago, Massachusetts citizens voted in favor of a referendum to lower property taxes. Our Massachusetts Council of Churches warned that the impact of the measure would be to drastically reduce the money available for services to the poor in our inner cities. But most suburban families thought the measure was sound because it meant personal savings for them. That was as far as they could see. One man remarked to me, for instance, that he was sorry the measure would adversely affect the poor. But he was voting for it anyway, he said, because the additional money in his pocket would ease the burden of his son's college tuition. Of course these are not easy times even for middle class people. Compared to the urban poor, however, we are very well off indeed. We read in Luke: "Everyone to whom much is given, of him will much be required." When we entered the voting booth, though, few of us troubled to ask: What will happen to the truly poor if I vote for my own pocketbook?

The same thing is happening at the national level as well. There, too, we are forcing the poor to take the brunt of economic sacrifice. In their recent book, *The New Class War,* Frances Piven and Richard Cloward show how vulnerable programs for the truly needy are. Food stamps, public housing, Aid to Families with Dependent Children, Medicaid, and CETA jobs have been eliminated with little opposition from the public. At the same time, however, welfare programs for the middle class family such as social security, college loans, and tax-deductible mortgages have been well defended. Thomas Jefferson said once that when he reflected God is just, he trembled for his country.

It was not some moralizing preacher but the century's most famous economist, Lord Keynes, who said: "The moral problem of our age is concerned with the love of money." In "Choruses from 'The Rock,'" T. S. Eliot asked:

> *When the Stranger says: 'What is the*
> *meaning of this city?*
> *Do you huddle close together because*
> *you love each other?'*

> *What will you answer? 'We all*
> *dwell together*
> *To make money from each other'? or*
> *'This is a community.'*

This is a good question for us. What is the meaning of our city? Is it meant merely to be an arena for merciless competition? Or is it intended for something more than that? Is our city meant to enjoy a spirit of merciful cooperation?

Modernity seems to have one answer to this question while the Gospel has another. As Jesus puts it, it is the difference between laying up treasures on earth and laying up treasures in heaven. We cannot have it both ways. "You cannot serve God and mammon," Jesus says.

The conventional wisdom in our consumer society is that life's end and happiness can be achieved by acquiring possessions. "Women," say our advertisements, "buy this perfume and you will find happiness with the man of your dreams." "Men, buy this car and women will compete ferociously for your attention." We sophisticated moderns tend to scorn the idol worshipers of antiquity, but really we have not progressed so very far. We are glad to bend the knee to some current incarnation of Baal, to some Gucci or Halston, say. While we Protestants are familiar with the great teaching of justification by grace through faith, we nevertheless attempt to justify our existence by building fancy houses and taking expensive vacations. Malcom Muggeridge was right to call ours the "Age of Credulity"!

Such a course is a dead end in every way. If we are looking to the things of this world to make us happy, we are looking in the wrong place, for as Yeats observed: "Everything that man esteems endures a moment or a day." It is interesting to me that cross-national surveys of rich and poor nations do not reveal striking differences in self-reported happiness. Egyptians are as happy as West Germans. Cubans are as happy as Americans.

The things of this world are powerless to bring us happiness. Worse still, they may even consume us. Few of us could feel secure in this life if we did not own some property. The problem comes when we center our lives around our possessions. Augustine said once: "We are our loves." By this logic, if we love our fine things, we ourselves will become a "thing." In fact this is happening. Erich Fromm remarked that "our industrial system is turning out machines that act like people and people that act like machines."

We say we are a consumer society, but really we are a consumed society. What we have has come to have us. Andrew Gide said that anything which we cannot give away really possesses us. In this "land of the free," we are not so free as we suppose. In nineteenth century England, the middle class was throwing off the yoke of the aristocracy and beginning to prosper mightily. Then a dour but insightful Scot named Thomas Carlyle reminded them in *Past and Present:*

> *The liberty of not being oppressed by your fellow men is an indispensable, yet one of the most insignificant, fractional parts of human liberty. Thou art the thrall not of Cedric the Saxon, but of thy own brutal appetites. And thou pratest of thy liberty? Thou entire blockhead.*

Yes, we are blockheads, but we are not "entire" blockheads. In Tolstoi's *Anna Karenina,* an old peasant explains to Konstantin Levin why a certain man is good with the words: "He lives for his soul, he remembers God." At least we know how perishable our souls are, and so we come here today to "remember" God and who he calls us to be. We come to listen to a gospel of life and freedom, and God, we may be sure, will speak to us.

Jesus spoke often of the uselessness of trusting in things to provide our happiness. He was not indifferent to the material requirements of life, and he told his followers to pray for their daily bread. But he realized that we can be happy only when we follow God's intention for us. Architects like Frank Lloyd Wright have said that a building's form must reflect its function; something of this principle holds true for our lives. God has made us for himself, that we might glorify him by deeds of service. That is our function, and if we would be happy, then the form of our lives must correspond to it. Isaiah said: "If you pour yourself out for the hungry and satisfy the desire of the afflicted, then shall your light rise in the darkness and your gloom be as the noonday."

This is what Jesus had in mind when he spoke of laying up treasures in heaven. There is nothing ethereal or vague about his admonition. In the context of his overall teachings, Jesus' imperative can be seen to have concrete implications for our behavior.

Consider, for example, the parable of the Good Samaritan which Jesus relates in the course of a discussion with a lawyer who asks what he must do to inherit eternal life. Think, if you will, of the various travelers as they came upon the beaten man. Now what do you suppose was in their minds? I imagine the priest and Levite passed by because their question was different from the Samaritan's. The priest and Levite must have wondered: What will happen to me if I stop? Will I have to inconvenience myself? Might I even be in danger? The Samaritan, though, must have thought to himself: What will happen to this poor man if I do not help him? This, I think, is the mark of people who lay up treasure in heaven. They are willing to risk themselves for others, even as God himself became vulnerable by taking human form and going to the cross.

An old rabbinical story amplifies this point. Rabbi Wolf was a just man. One day Mrs. Wolf cried out that her maid had stolen a valuable object. The servant, a poor orphan, tearfully denied the charge.

"We will let the Rabbinical Court settle this!" declared the Rabbi's wife. When Rabbi Wolf saw her preparing to go to court, he began to put on his Sabbath robe.

"Why do you do that?" she indignantly asked. "You know it is unseemly for a man of your position to come to court with me. I can very well plead my own case."

"I am sure you can," answered the Rabbi. "But who will plead the case of your maid, the poor orphan? I must see that full justice be done to her."

What does it mean to lay up treasures in heaven? One thing it means is to evaluate public policy not so much in terms of its impact upon us as its effect upon the disadvantaged. The message of the parable of the Good Samaritan is that we owe these people something, even if it is personally disadvantageous to us. Then we can say in response to Eliot's question: "This is a community."

Lent is speaking to us now, calling us to repentance. There is nothing easy about repentance. Jesus said: "Where your treasure is, there will be your heart." If we have invested our energies and ambitions in the things of this world, then we will have become "slaves to our brutal appetites."

Yet I take some measure of hope from these words of our Lord. The order of the phrasing here is significant, I think. Notice that Jesus does not say: Where your heart is, there will be your treasure. Instead he says: "Where your treasure is, there will be your heart." We are used to thinking, of course, that thoughts and feelings determine actions and not the other way around. We say, for example, "I felt like doing it," as if it is the feeling that gives rise to the act. We know how very stubborn feelings can be. If our fine possessions have captured our affections, then our liberation would not seem to be in the offing. If we are going to wait for our feelings or thinking to change, then we are going to wait for a very long time indeed.

But Jesus says: "Where your treasure is, there will be your heart." To my mind, the ordering of our Lord's words raises the possibility that feelings and thoughts do not so much determine actions as actions determine feelings and thoughts. If this is true, then there is hope for our liberation. Psychotherapists have learned that often it is easier to act your way into a new mode of feeling and thinking than it is to feel or think your way into a new mode of acting. This has led in bereavement counseling, for instance, to "action therapy" where a person is encouraged to do something about his situation whether he wants to or not.

In this Lenten season, then, I want to suggest that you begin to practice "action therapy" against what psychoanalyst Karen Horney said is the dominant neurosis of our day, "the wish to have everything." Take a careful look at your family budget. What does it say about your priorities? Are you amassing merely perishable treasure? If you are, try shifting your treasure from earth to heaven. Forego purchasing some non-essential item, that extra television or telephone or home video game or expensive ski trip. Don't think about it — just do it! Then use the savings to purchase a pearl of greater price by contributing to our United Church of Christ Hunger Action Fund, which combats hunger and poverty here and abroad. That would be a Lenten sacrifice which counts for something. By doing this you will begin to experience a new sense of freedom. You will be emboldened to make additional sacrifices of non-essentials and your values will become more like those of Jesus himself. We should sacrifice not until it hurts, but until it begins to feel good and we come to see it is no sacrifice at all. We should come at last to understand with Plato that, "True poverty consists not in the decrease of one's possessions, but in the increase of one's greed."

In the opinion of Gibbon, what destroyed Rome was the disintegration of family life within the home, not the power of the enemy without the gate. America's families are disintegrating, and by this I have more in mind than just the divorce statistics. So many of our families appear prosperous when really they know the meanest poverty, the poverty of a weary spirit, the poverty which issues from laying up treasures on earth. One of America's most distinguished family therapists, Virginia Satir, says that families which are truly nurturing to their members are always "linked to society in an open and hopeful way." If love is limited to the narrow confines of the family, it is dangerous, as the case of Montegrano demonstrates so vividly. To be sure, we are responsible to our families, but we are responsible as well to our country and to all humankind.

What about your own family? Is it a center for moral education? We teach our children to read and compute before they go to school. Do we equip them also with values to give their lives meaning and purpose when they go into the world? Are you teaching your children by example what it means to lay up treasures in heaven? We frequently say that our family's happiness is our primary concern. If we truly want our families to be happy, then we will do the word of the Lord. "Blessed are those who hunger and thirst for righteousness," he said. "For they shall be satisfied."

# Free and Faithful

## FIRST SUNDAY IN LENT
### Matthew 4:1-11

*Then Jesus was led up by the Spirit into the wilderness to be tempted . . .*

— Matthew 4:1

In Huxley's *Brave New World,* Savage is contending with Mustapha Mond, the world controller. Savage's sensibility has been shaped by the Bible and Shakespeare, readings no longer allowed to the public. He complains to Mond about the antiseptic quality of life in the new society. The controller says to him: "We prefer to do things comfortably." Savage rejoins: "But I don't want comfort. I want God, I want poetry, I want real danger, I want freedom, I want goodness. I want sin."

Many people think of God as a kind of cosmic Mustapha Mond or world controller. They have in mind a certain picture of God. It is one which most of us share in some measure, and one to which much of Holy Scripture points. This is the God who calls the worlds into being. The almighty God who, in the words of a great hymn, "alone can create and alone can destroy." The God who, in the words of Paul, "accomplishes all things according to the counsel of his will." The God who, as the popular song goes, "has the whole world in his hands." This is the God who on Easter morning brought life out of death; the God who is in control of our destiny and whose will is invincible.

But we must permit this picture of God to be qualified and enlarged by another. There is another picture of God which reveals that his preferences are like those of Savage himself, a picture which suggests that God does not want easy comfort for his creatures, but prefers freedom, goodness, and sin. This picture is drawn, for example, in the Revelation of St. John with his vision of the Christ who says: "Behold, I stand at the door and knock; if anyone hears my voice, I will come into him." The accent here is not on God's power but on human freedom, freedom to accept or reject God, to choose goodness or sin. It is an accent we find also near the beginning of Scripture, in Deuteronomy, where we read: "I am setting before you this day the ways of life and death." Life or death, happiness or misery — it's your choice.

Right through the Bible, then, we have a picture of a God who is almighty, but who does not coerce his creatures. Instead he permits them to choose their own way and to live with the consequences. When I was in England last, I saw a painting at Oxford which continues to haunt me. It was done by the artist Holman Hunt in the last century. It is a picture of Christ standing before a closed door, looking forsaken and disconsolate with a crown of thorns on his brow. The door before him is shut so hard and fast that the brush and vines have grown up across it. Yes, God is great, the maker of heaven and earth. But we are powerful, too, because God has given us the freedom to shut him out from our souls and from our world.

Why does God make us such a gift of freedom? George MacDonald, the nineteenth century Scottish divine, said:

*God wants to make us in his own image, choosing the good, refusing the evil. How should he effect this if he were always moving us from within towards the beauty of his holiness?*

God, you see, loves us and wants nothing more than for us to love him and to choose the good. But he will not for us. Love which is coerced is not love at all. I think married couples and old friends grasp this fact intuitively. If I thought, for example, that Beverly's parents had forced her to marry me, well then, no matter what she might say, I would spend much of my time wondering what was in her own heart. If I had reason to believe her love for me was not genuine, then our relationship would be a burden rather than a source of strength and joy. Something of this principle holds true, I believe, for relationships between God and his creatures. God wants our love, but not just on any terms. He wants it freely and happily given, or he wants it not at all. Only in that way can we become his genuine partner.

It is in this context that we need to consider the story of Jesus' temptations. In the beginning of his ministry, Jesus had to decide how he would reveal himself as God's Messiah. He might have revealed himself in such a way as to compel people's allegiance and eliminate human freedom. If he had turned the stones to bread, or jumped from the temple without injury, or become a political deliverer, then people would have had no choice but to recognize him and follow him. If he had performed the miracles demanded by the devil, he could have guaranteed people's loyalty.

Jesus chose to reject these possibilities, however. He saw them as temptations of the devil. He understood that what was threatened was the character of faith itself, faith as a free response to God's love. We are accustomed to saying: Seeing is believing. But Christian faith is a matter of believing or trusting even without seeing. "Blessed are those who have not seen and yet believe," the resurrected Jesus tells his disciples. "Faith," writes the author of Hebrews, "is the conviction of things unseen, the assurance of things hoped for." This is why in the second chapter of John's Gospel, we see Jesus withdrawing from the crowd which believes only because of the signs he works. Faith which demands a sign is not faith at all.

This insight is beautifully captured by the Catholic writer Graham Greene in his most recent novel: *Monsignor Quixote.* Father Quixote is troubled by a nightmare in which Christ is saved from the cross by a legion of angels, and the whole world knows for sure that he is the Son of God. He whispers to himself: "There was no ambiguity, no room for doubt, and no room for faith at all. God save me from such a belief."

So we are called to choose for or against God, but we find the act of choosing to be hard. Even in life's smallest things, we find it hard to make decisions sometimes. For example, the other evening after I returned from a long meeting, Beverly and I tried to plan our schedules for the coming week. On one particular evening, we had been asked to do four different things. "What should we do?" she asked me. "I don't know," I said. "I'm too tired to decide. You choose." This was a minor matter, of course, but I think much of life is like that. Our freedom to choose becomes burdensome, and we are eager to forfeit it.

If small choices can be burdensome, how much more difficult are those decisions which decide our ultimate destiny! This is the point of Dostoevski's terrifying parable about the Grand Inquisitor in *The Brothers Karamazov.* Christ is imagined as returning to sixteenth century Seville. The Grand Inquisitor, acting for the Church, marches him off to prison. He charges Christ with having placed upon humankind the unbearable burden of freedom. By resisting the Tempter in the wilderness, Christ made people miserable rather than happy. By refusing to make visible his power, Christ laid upon people the necessity of choosing for or against God, not on the basis of some handy empirical data, but in faith alone. People were sorely oppressed by this freedom, and the Church was correcting Jesus' work. The Church was assuming the burden of freedom and exercising in its place its own severe authority, relieving people of their responsibility to choose for or against God. Dostoevski concluded his parable with frightening words:

> *And the people rejoiced that they were again led like sheep and that the terrible gift that brought them such suffering (freedom) was at last lifted from their hearts.*

I think we are all a bit like the people in Dostoevski's story. God means us to be free, but sometimes we stagger under the weight of our freedom. We do not receive our freedom as a gift. Instead we ask God for a sign. We demand nothing so dramatic as turning stone to bread, perhaps, but still we ask for a sign. We are a bit like Jacob who, after his experience at Bethel, made a vow saying:

> *"If God will be with me and will keep me in this way that I go, and will give me bread to eat and clothing to wear, so that I come again to my father's house in peace, **then** the Lord shall be my God."*

We are just like that at times. How many people have said on their hospital bed, for example, that if God will make them well, then they will become active in the work of the church? We often try to force God to show himself in a clear, unmistakable way. This is why I am not surprised by the perennial hardiness of fundamentalist religion which offers its believers absolute and total certainty. Freedom can be a fearful burden, and so there will always be people looking to follow some Grand Inquisitor.

As Paul writes to Galatia, though, we have been called to freedom, and in freedom we must stand fast. If we understand this, then we can begin to understand the position our church takes on some controversial social issues. Our commitment to liberty is the reason, for example, why many clergy of mainline denominations favor freedom of choice in the matter of abortion. We are not indifferent to the moral issues of abortion, but we are sensitive to the moral issue of freedom. God has made us free, and it is a dangerous matter to permit government policy to usurp God's gift of freedom. This is also why so many religious leaders are opposed to religious observances in our public schools. Given the power of peer pressure, it is dubious that school prayer can ever be truly voluntary; prayer which does not issue from genuine freedom is less than what God actually requires of us.

We dare not forfeit our spiritual freedom, for to lose that is to lose our souls as well. To borrow a phrase from an ancient Church Father, God has made this world to be a place for "soul-making." God in his love, wisdom, and providence provides many opportunities for us to choose ways which are at odds with his own. These temptations are vexing to us, and yet we should see them not as obstacles to our faith, but rather as the means by which our faith may be upbuilt. God intends for us, in the words of Ephesians, to attain to "mature manhood, to the measure of the fullness of Christ." As P. T. Forsyth observed: "The way to the soul's final greatness lies through its misery rather than through its success." It lies through the misery of those hard choices we are called to make about our life and destiny.

God means for us to be free, truly free, because faith

can be real only where faithlessness is a possibility. Faith can be real, then, only in a world of temptations. This is why in our lesson Matthew emphasizes it was the Spirit of God himself which led Jesus into the wilderness to be tempted. Centuries earlier, in a similar way, God led his people Israel into temptation. We read in Deuteronomy:

> *"The Lord your God led you forty years in the wilderness, that he might humble you, testing you to know . . . whether you would keep his commandments or not."*

Then, too, in his First Epistle, Peter wrote to Christians who were tempted to return to Judaism, who were exposed to the contempt and abuse of those who had not been converted. Peter said to them:

> *. . . you may have to suffer various trials so that the genuineness of your faith, more precious than gold, which though perishable is tested by fire, may redound to praise and glory and honor at the revelation of Jesus Christ.*

If we are to become vessels of faith, instruments which God can use, we need first to be forged and tested in a crucible, in the crucible of freedom and choice. It is in this way, as George MacDonald observed, that we are made in God's image, choosing the good, refusing the evil.

The crucible is no less terrible for Christians today than it was for those of Peter's time. We live in a pagan culture. There is a constant temptation for us to fall away from our faith toward the prevailing hedonism. There is a steady temptation to go after the great gods of pleasure and materialism. We have our choices to make! But do you know something? This fact should not discourage us. Instead, it should hearten us. It means not only that we are free to reject God, but that we also are free to choose God, even amidst those forces which prey upon life.

This is one meaning of a moving story related by Elie Wiesel. He tells of a teacher, a just man, who came to Sodom, determined to save its inhabitants from sin and punishment. Night and day he walked the streets and the markets protesting against greed and theft, falsehood and indifference. In the beginning, people listened and smiled ironically; then they stopped listening, and he no longer even amused them. The killers went on killing; the wise kept silent, as if there were no just men in their midst. One day a child, moved by compassion for the unfortunate teacher, approached him with these words: "You shout, you scream. Don't you see that it is hopeless?" "Yes, I see," answered the just man. "Then why do you go on?"

"I'll tell you why," said the just man. "In the beginning I thought I could change them; today I know that I cannot. If I still shout today, if I still scream, and I scream louder and louder, stronger and stronger, it is to prevent them from ultimately changing me."

In this world where the darkness seems so impenetrable, we may nevertheless choose the good and refuse the evil. Let us rejoice, then, that in God's gift of freedom, we have no mean burden but instead the chance to become the best we can be. God has graced us with the freedom to be ourselves, his own blessed children.

# A Book Which Reads Us

**SECOND SUNDAY IN LENT**
**John 4:5-26 (27-30, 39-42)**

*"Come, see a man who told me all that I ever did."*
— John 4:29

Hans-Ruedi Weber relates a story which is often told in East Africa. A simple woman always walked around with her bulky Bible. She never was parted from it. So the villagers began to tease her: "Why always the Bible?" they asked. "There are so many other books you could read." Yet the woman kept on living with her Bible, neither disturbed nor angered by all the teasing. But finally one day, she knelt down in the midst of those who laughed at her. She held up the Bible, high above her head, and said with a great smile: "Yes, of course there are many books which I could read. Yet there is only one book which reads me."

I thought of this story as I read of the encounter between Jesus and the Samaritan woman. How improbable a meeting it must have seemed to Jesus' disciples. Jews were contemptuous of Samaritans. Rabbis avoided speaking to women in public. But with his customary disdain for the national and sexual chauvinism of his day, Jesus spoke to this woman, and he graced her.

Remember, now, that this was a woman who was living with a man without benefit of clergy and who had been married five times. We may suppose she had led an emotionally rending life and that she bore the scars of marital rejection. Victor Hugo said the supreme happiness of life is the conviction that we are loved; by this standard, the Samaritan woman must have been a supremely unhappy person. Then, one day, a man came along who was a Jew and a Rabbi to boot. No doubt she fully expected him to snub her. But instead he engaged her, not just superficially, but to her very depths. He measured both the poverty and the requirement of her life. The love in his eyes and the concern in his voice emboldened her, dejected and cynical though she must have been, to cry out once more for acceptance and care. She said: "Sir, give me this water, that I may not thirst, nor come here to draw." Jesus gave her himself. The hopes and fears of all her years were met in the Christ, in that incarnation of God's love whom she there beheld. Jesus read her, her sorrow and her need, like a book. When she went back to her town, she could say to the people there: "Come, see a man who told me all that I ever did."

Pastors are always admonishing their congregations to read and study the Bible, but that simple African woman grasped the very genius of Scripture when she suggested that really, it is the Bible which reads us. As the Samaritan woman learned, encounters with the living Christ are really exercises in self-discovery. The Bible is not so much about exotic places and peoples as it is about you and me. It is about and for people who have experienced what Melville called the "damp, drizzly November of the soul." Its message fills our empty places with love, love which comes not because of what we have done or what we are in the eyes of the world, but love which is on the house, which is unconditional, there for you or for me or for anyone at all just to grab as God gives it away. "God so loved the world," we read, "that he gave his only son, that whoever believes in him should not perish but have eternal life.'' This single line from John is the Christian gospel, Martin Luther said. The gospel for "whoever," a gift to anyone whose life has rough and heartrending edges. It assures us we cannot move beyond God's love and compassion. To know this, to feel this in the recesses of our hearts and minds is, as Hugo said, to be supremely happy. In Dag Hammarskjold's words, it is to be "illumined by the steady radiance, renewed daily, of a wonder, the source of which is beyond all reason."

This is why I am sorry for people who say we should read the Bible as we would any other literature. As Frederick Buechner observes in *Wishful Thinking:*

> *The advice has a pleasantly modern and reasonable ring to it. Read the Bible for the story it tells. Read the King James version for the power of its prose and the splendour of its poetry. Read it for the history it contains and for its insights into ancient ways. Don't worry about whatever it is supposed to mean to religious faith . . . Read it like any other book. The trouble is it is not like any other book. To read the Bible as literature is like reading Moby Dick as a whaling manual.*

The Bible is not just another noble chapter in our literary history. As no other book does, it tells us who we are and whose we are. It is not so much a book which we read, as a book which reads us.

To read the Bible is to embark on a voyage of self-discovery. This is why the Bible remains important even in the twentieth century. It often is said that we live in a secular culture, that religion is on the wane, and that the Bible's significance has declined. This is sheer nonsense! In some quarters the institutional church may be on the wane, but the search for meaning and purpose, which is at the heart of religious life, is conducted as feverishly today as ever. There are many signs of this in our culture.

Look, for example, at our films. Many of them have as their theme "adventure in outer space." Think of them all: "Close Encounters"; "Star Wars" I and II; "Star Trek"; and so on. Why are we so preoccupied with worlds beyond our own? Are we merely curious about our material universe? Or does our interest suggest something profound about the needs of our hearts and minds? Some thirty years ago, Carl Jung, the great psychoanalyst, tried to explain why so many people were fascinated by UFO phenomena. He wrote: "We are all born to believe. The eyes may be wrong, but the psyche is right. We are all looking for a perfect model of ourselves." C. S. Lewis made the same point when he observed:

> *Most people, if they had really learned to look into their own hearts, would know that they do want, and want acutely, something that cannot be had in this world. There are all sorts of things in this world that offer to give it to you, but they never quite keep their promise. The longings which arise in us when we first fall in love, or first think of some foreign country, or first take up some subject that excites us, are longings which no marriage, no travel, no learning can really satisfy. I am not now speaking of what would ordinarily be called unsuccessful marriages, or holidays, or learned careers. I am speaking of the best possible ones. There was something we grasped at, in that first moment of longing, which just fades away in reality. I think everyone knows what I mean. The wife may be a good wife, and the hotels and scenery may have been excellent, and chemistry may be a very*

*interesting job, but something has evaded us.*
(quoted in *The Joyful Christian*)

So we look to other worlds.

"E. T." is one of the most successful movies of all time. It is about an extra-terrestrial creature who heals cuts with the touch of his finger, raises dead flowers to life, and who himself is raised from the dead before he departs earth, his spaceship leaving a rainbow in the sky. I would guess that millions of people who never enter the door of a church have flocked to "E. T." and been moved by it. They are searching for a source of hope. They are looking for a model of themselves as people who are loved by a power which will not let them go even in their darkness. So much, then, for the claim that modernity has numbed the religious nerve!

Much of what we see happening about us reflects a widespread failure to find an adequate model for living. This is true, for example, of our number one social problem, alcohol abuse. We are all troubled by the many teenagers who drink and drive with such devastating consequences to themselves and others. Across the country there are moves afoot in state legislatures to raise the drinking age and to stiffen sentences for drunk drivers. These moves will probably help, and I am all for them. But you know, they do not even begin to address the underlying problem. That problem cannot be legislated away. Our real problem is the materialism which dominates and stifles our culture, which breeds meaninglessness and loneliness. This environment is shriveling up the souls of our young people, painfully, and they are using alcohol as an anaesthetic. In Tolstoi's *The Death of Ivan Illyich,* Ivan could resist the pain of his cancer as long as he believed his life had meaning. When he lost a sense of meaning, however, he could only scream. When teenagers repeatedly get drunk, they are really screaming. They are crying: Does anybody care about me? Does life really matter? Does it matter to anyone what I am doing? Am I loved?

In the Gospel of Christ the Church has an answer to these questions. We have just the word which this world groaning in travail needs to hear, word of God's unconditional love revealed once and for all in his son. What is so sad is that the world does not know that we have what it is looking for. What is sadder still is the fact that this is largely our own fault.

Rather than proclaim Christ's gospel of love and acceptance, the Church too often settles for being the enforcer of some narrow social convention or theological dogma. James Knight was a Navy chaplain in World War II. On Wake Island, he tried to minister to an American engineer who was dying from tuberculosis. The man said to Knight: "I am frightened and alone. I have no philosophy of life adequate for living and dying. I always went to church and was reared in a religious home. But all I was given in church was a series of negatives — don't do this, don't do that — about smoking, dancing and card playing, and other forms of social activity. In prison camp, where I remained for almost four years, I had no philosophy for living, and now I have no philosophy for dying." How miserably the Church failed that man! In all his years of church-going, he seems never to have heard the Good News.

This morning I simply say: What about you and me and this church in Shrewsbury? Are we like that African woman who carried her Bible with her everywhere she went? Are we like her — sustained by God's word in all times and in all places? Have we allowed the Bible to read us, to fathom us in all the unlovely places of our lives as Jesus did that woman of Samaria? Have we permitted God's grace to permeate our sadness with the unshakable conviction that we nonetheless are loved?

As we move about this troubled world, what of God's love we are able to share with people who lead lives of quiet desperation? When people look at us, when they look at this church, what do they see? Is our very life a proclamation, a living word for God? Do we, by our active presence, grace those about us with love and concern, as Jesus did that woman by the well?

To borrow an image from Martin Luther, are you on the way to becoming a "little Christ"? Are you?

# Out of the Darkness

## THIRD SUNDAY IN LENT
## John 9:1-41

*". . . I am the light of the world."*

— John 9:5

St. Augustine wrote of our lesson: "This blind man stands for the human race . . . if the blindness is infidelity, then the illumination is faith." Surely we need the illumination of Christian faith today. Ours is one of those epochs of which it may be said, as Shakespeare said of Romeo, "affliction is enamoured of thy parts . . . and thou art wedded to calamity."

Worse still, we seem bereft of a vision to sustain us. "Without a vision, the people perish," declares the biblical proverb. It seemed to T. S. Eliot on the eve of the Second World War that the people were perishing because they had no vision:

*They all go into the dark . . .*
*The captains, merchant bankers, eminent men of*
*    letters,*
*The generous patrons of art, the statesmen and*
*    rulers,*
*Distinguished civil servants, chairmen of many*
*    committees,*
*Industrial lords and petty contractors, all go into*
*    the dark,*
*And dark the Sun and Moon, and the Almanach*
*    de Gotha*

*And the Stock Exchange Gazette, the Directory*
*of Directors,*
*And cold the sense and lost the motive of action.*

From a glance at our morning paper, it seems today that we are paralyzed and perishing. We are in the dark and need desperately to be baptized with a vision of who we might become.

In our lesson, the blind man is healed when he washes in the pool of Siloam, the name of which means "one who is sent." In this way John identifies the pool of water with Christ. Jesus is the one sent by the Father to be the light of the world and to open wide the blind eyes of humanity. Jesus is the enfleshment of God's own eternal vision of shalom, or peace, God's dream that all things in heaven and on earth will be reunited. I want this morning to speak concretely about God's vision as it has been revealed in Christ. I want to speak of it in the context of two issues which press upon our consciences: capital punishment and the nuclear freeze. These are related issues and they are as much religious as political matters. They bear materially upon God's creation.

Please undertand that I do not speak ex cathedra; I shall try not to dogmatize like some infallible know-it-all. I do think that faithful Christians will examine all public issues in the light of Christ's gospel; but I also think that faithful Christians can disagree in their conclusions. While I speak with conviction this morning and will mince no words, I will not presume to question your own faithfulness if you disagree with me. That would be the height of arrogance, and I do not want to stand with the Pharisee in the temple. What is interesting to me, however, is the near unanimous opposition by mainline Protestant, Catholic, and Jewish leaders around the country to the reinstatement of the death penalty and their widespread endorsement of a nuclear freeze. Of course this does not mean that people in the pew have to hold the same views, but I think you will agree that you need at least to take them seriously.

Let me begin my analysis of capital punishment by saying I believe retribution is a legitimate aspect of punishment. I do not agree with those church people who say that retribution implies vindictiveness. I think wrongdoers deserve to suffer and that punishment is a necessary step toward their reformation. If a crime has been a terrible one, the penalty should reflect that.

But in this regard, let us try to set aside all the emotional arguments that encircle the issue, and let us try instead to set out some Christian principles. Of course this is no easy thing to do. The Bible is not a manual of applied ethics, and it is not always so easy to discern what biblical principles are relevant or how they faithfully may be applied. As Nathaniel Micklem said: "God speaks to us through the Bible's words, but we cannot without thinking apply these words to our immediate questions. We are given a compass, not a map." Yet it seems to me that in the matter of capital punishment, the compass points more clearly than it does for some other issues.

The first thing we need to know is that contrary to some popular opinion, there is no blanket endorsement of capital punishment in our Bible, not even in the Old Testament. Not even in the passage we have in Deuteronomy which says: "It shall be life for life, eye for eye, tooth for tooth, hand for hand, foot for foot." This does sound at first like a prescription for vengeance. But that is only because so many modern readers of the Bible do not understand the ancient historical context. Originally, the "eye for an eye" was not a green light for revenge, but it was a stop light to mark the limits of retaliation. This law of an eye for an eye actually showed great concern for the guilty party by limiting retaliation. You see in ancient times, a man who lost one eye might retaliate by poking out both eyes of the guilty party. Or the friends of someone who was killed might respond by not only killing the murderer but his entire family as well. Old Testament law was concerned to put a brake on this barbarism. There is no prohibition against vengeance here, as we have later in Jesus' own teachings, but even in Deuteronomy there is an attempt to limit violence.

Most important, though, when the state sanctions the death penalty, it denies one of the most basic principles of the Judaeo-Christian tradition. It is a principle which is central to Christ's gospel and particularly to our Lenten season. It is the principle that people can repent and their lives can be redeemed. We read in Ezekiel's prophecy: "Have I any pleasure at all that the wicked should die? saith the Lord God, and not that he should return from his ways and live?" Wrongdoers need to be punished. They need to be forced to consider the brutality of their deeds so that they can repent of their sin and be restored to communion with their Creator and their brothers and sisters. Quick, stiff sentencing to prison makes repentance possible; but the death penalty eliminates all possiblity of the reclamation of life. This is foolish as well as faithless, for the religious community knows that repentance is possible on the basis of its own tradition. Repentance turned a murderer named Moses into the deliverer of a great nation. Repentance turned a bigot named Paul into the greatest apostle of the Christian faith. A few summers ago in a federal prison, I did transactional analysis therapy with some men convicted of armed robbery. Through their experiences in Yokefellows, a religious organization for prisoners, two of them have come into a profound relationship with Christ. They are serving now as valuable assistants to the prison chaplain.

I am not an exceptionally obstinate man, but there is only one way you could change my mind about capital punishment. That is, if you could convince me that the death penalty has a deterrent effect, that by reinstating the measure, we could prevent some future violent crime and save innocent life. For only then would you have an ethical case to go against the one I have outlined. Sometimes, in some cases, Christians have a responsibility to restrain evil if they are able. This is why many men interrupted their divinity studies during World War II and took up arms. They were aware of Jesus' teachings about the use of force, but they believed there was also a moral imperative to restrain the evil of demonic fascism. Sometimes in this fallen world, moral decisionmaking involves choosing between two evils, and determining which is the lesser wrong. If you could prove to me that capital punishment has a deterrent effect, that it would restrain murder, then I would reconsider my view. But, as you know, the evidence here is conflicting and inconclusive. Indeed, Professor Bowers of Northeastern University has research to show that violent crime actually increases after an execution.

There is one more thing. It is the fact that capital punishment is really a political smokescreen. It misleads the public about the causes of crime and about meaningful deterrents to criminal activity. All of us are concerned about the rising tide of crime. We mourn the agonies of the victims and their survivors. But capital punishment does not address the real issue.

What is the real issue? Consider the people who sit on death row. Who are they? By and large they are poor white people, Blacks, Hispanics, and native Americans. They are all the have-nots who continue to suffer from bigotry in an economy which has no place for them. I do not mean to say this relieves them of moral responsibility for their deeds. It does not. But really, what do we expect? We know perfectly well that cruel poverty breeds desperation, and that desperation in turn breeds crime. The real issue is that this country has failed to address the causes of poverty.

Which brings me at last to the nuclear freeze. President Eisenhower made this connection between poverty and crime and the arms race explicit when he said:

> *Every gun that is made, every warship launched, every rocket fired signifies, in the final sense, a theft from those who hunger and are not fed . . . and those who are cold and are not clothed. This world in arms is not spending money alone. It is spending the sweat of its labors and the hopes of its children. This is not a way of life at all in any true sense. It is humanity hanging from a cross of iron.*

The nuclear freeze movement calls upon the United States government to work vigorously to negotiate a mutual, verifiable weapons moratorium and reduction with the Soviet Union. With the spirit of General Eisenhower, we must begin to dismantle the nuclear "cross of iron" so that we may begin to use our resources to reduce the dreadful poverty which gives rise to crime. As the General said, you cannot produce peace with hate and a club. A strong defense is necessary, but strong social and economic structures are just as important. Of course, we want the world to be safe for democracy. But we would like to be safe in our homes and on our streets as well.

Samuel Willard, the Congregationalist divine who preached the Election Sermon to the assembled magistrates in Boston in 1682, said on that occasion: "If the rulers of the Bay Colony can tolerate the dishonor of Christ, let me boldly say, I believe he will soon and signally testify his dislike of it." I would amend Willard's words only a bit this morning. I believe Christ is already testifying, not in some mystical or abstract way, but in the decay and decline of a once great people now paralyzed by fear which issues from blindness. The face of Jesus Christ is brooding over this country, as long ago he brooded over Jerusalem, and he will not permit himself to be spat upon or crowned with thorns for very much longer. Christ is brooding over this land because too many of its people have affirmed not a Christian vision of life, hope, love, and peace, but have affirmed instead a demonic vision of legalized murder, exploitation, and war. So, as you leave this place, remember how a man of God once said to the ancient Hebrew assembly: "I am giving you this day a choice between life and death, between God's blessing and God's curse. And I call heaven and earth to witness the choice you make."

Remember that. And then choose life!

# Claim Your Ministry

## FOURTH SUNDAY IN LENT
## Matthew 20:17-28

*"but whoever would be great among you must be your servant."*

— Matthew 20:26b

Augustine wrote: "So deep has human pride sunk us that only divine humility can raise us." This point was not lost on St. Martin, the famous soldier-saint of France. The story goes that one day he was praying and there appeared to him a figure robed like a king with a jeweled crown and gold-embroidered shoes. The voice said to him: "Martin, recognize him whom you see. I am Christ. I am about to descend to the earth and I am showing myself to you first." A couple of minutes later, the voice went on: "Why do you hesitate, Martin, to believe me? I am Christ." Martin replied: "The Lord Jesus did not foretell that he would come in purple and crowned in gold. I will not believe that Christ is come unless I see him in the dress and in the form in which he suffered." At that point the figure disappeared, and Martin realized it was a temptation of the devil.

We often speak of the "glory" of Christ. We do not so often remember that Christ, by his death on the cross, has infused the word with new meaning. Christ's glory is not that of some potentate or tycoon. As Isaac Watts wrote:

*But in the grace that rescu'd man,*
    *His brightest form of glory shines;*
*Here, on the cross, 'tis fairest drawn*
    *In precious blood, and crimson lines.*

I said this point was not lost on St. Martin. But it has been lost on many of our Lord's followers who were not so eager to serve as to engage in one-upsmanship. In our lesson today, for example, we see the sons of Zebedee avidly contending for first place in the heavenly sweepstakes. So Jesus says to them:

*"You know the rulers of the Gentiles lord it over them, and their great men exercise authority over them. It shall not be so among you; but whoever would be great among you must be your servant, and whoever would be first among you must be your slave; even as the Son of man came not to be served but to serve, and to give his life as a ransom for many."*

This must have been a hard saying for James and John, and it is no easier for us. Even in the Church there are people who try to lord it over others in a way that Jesus never did. Indeed within our churches we often find such patterns of dominance and submission to be institutionalized. This is the issue I address today.

We need to begin by remembering that the ministry of the Church is committed to each and every one of us and to all of us together. In his First Epistle, Peter borrows language applied by the Old Testament to ancient Israel, and he uses it to describe the ministry which we share. He says to the Church of his own day and to ours:

*You are a chosen race, a royal priesthood, a holy nation, God's own people, that you may declare*

*the wonderful deeds of him who called you out
of darkness into his marvelous light.*

Peter makes no distinction between clergy and laity. He
does not say that some of us are priests, but he says that
all of us together are a royal priesthood. We are meant
to be a community of people who worshipfully make
God central in our lives and use our gifts for the service
of men and women. "You are a royal priesthood,"
Peter says to all of us.

But in subsequent centuries that imperative was
obscured, and complex orders of clergy emerged. By the
sixteenth century, the clergy had become the ruling class
of the Church, and for all practical purposes they were
considered to be the Church. It even became
unnecessary to have a congregation in order to celebrate
the Mass. But the Protestant Reformation led by Martin
Luther recovered the New Testament conception that
the priesthood is committed to all believers. Luther said
that we are all baptized into the ministry and that laity
should have a role in Church government. Then John
Calvin, a generation later, called not only for lay
participation in Church government, but for a vital
sense of lay ministry in the worlds of work, politics,
education, and family life.

Of course the Reformers did not abolish the clergy.
They believed that in order to overcome ignorance of
faith and superstition about religious matters, the
Church must insist on clarity of preaching and teaching
about the gospel; they delegated the ministry of Word
and Sacrament to those whose calling and education
prepared them for this task. But what they did abolish
was the distinction between clergy rulers, on the one
hand, and lay subjects on the other. When they
ordained candidates to the ministry of Word and
Sacrament, they did not presume to think they thereby
conferred some special grace or status or power on their

clergy. Instead, they understood ordination to be a rite of the Church whereby some members of the body were appointed to special tasks. In the way that the arm or hand or tongue labors for the body in its specific way, so too, these members were to labor for the Church in the specific tasks of preaching and teaching.

Indeed, so far from the medieval notion of clergy rule was the Protestant conception of ministry that Calvin could say the act of ordination should be looked upon as one of the principal modes employed by God to school men in humility. The Reformers believed that all ministry derived from God who was present in Christ, the great high priest. So, when they looked for models for ministry, they looked to the life of Christ. They understood from Scripture that Jesus had for all time defined the shape of ministry by his own sacrifice and by his word to the sons of Zebedee: "I am among you as one who serves." The Reformers grasped that Jesus was a king who had turned this world's understanding of kingship on its head by emptying himself, taking the form of a servant and leaving the royal robes in the closet. To this they drew a corollary, that their king's royal priesthood must share his qualities, that servanthood must define the shape of the Christian community, and that its leaders must be servants of the servants of God.

It is asked by churches which practice apostolic succession: What is the authority for the ministry of the Reformed churches? They point to the fact that all of their priests have been ordained by bishops who were ordained by bishops and so on in a continuous line all the way back to St. Peter. In this way, they believe, special priestly gifts have been transmitted from generation to generation. In answer to their question, our tradition responds that the ultimate authority of its ministry, clergy and lay, has the same basis as did the authority of the first generation of apostles — the authority of lives devoted in service to their Master. We read in the Acts of the Apostles that when the Christian group at Antioch sent representatives to a meeting of church leaders in Jerusalem, it sent with them a letter which read: "It seemed good to us to choose men who have risked their lives for the sake of our Lord Jesus Christ." As Halford Luccock reminded us, those early Christians grasped the very genius of the Christian gospel. "Here," they wrote, "are men who have risked their lives." That now, as then, is the final authority of Christianity in its appeal to the world. It is the final authority of discipleship, the ultimate credential of all ministry. It is the proof of the cross, of lives given entirely to their Master in a service. There is no other comparable authority for ministry. There never has been and there never will be. It was the original authority of Jesus who said he had come to give his life as a ransom for many. It is the authority of the humble servant.

This is what it means to be a royal priest of the great high priest. "I have given you an example," Jesus said after washing the feet of his disciples, "that you also should do as I have done to you." Paul wrote to the Ephesians that there are many gifts and ministries, but they all have a common denominator. They all are grounded in the ministry of Christ who took the form of a servant. Paul wrote to Philippi: "Have this mind among yourselves which you have in Christ Jesus, who, though he was in the form of God, emptied himself, and took the form of a servant." To understand this is to have a ministry no matter how small one's apparent gifts may be. To misunderstand this is to have no ministry. It matters not how great one's gifts are if they are not offered as Christ offered himself.

We have said a word about how our gifts are to be offered in ministry. Now let us say something about where they are to be used. It is important to offer our talents not only in the service of the church's committees and boards, but also at our workplace, at home, and in the wider world, wherever we are. Martin Luther said:

*If you are a craftsman, you will find the Bible placed in your workshop, in your hands, in your heart; it teaches and preaches how you ought to treat your neighbor. Only look at your tools, your needle, your thimble, your beer barrel, your articles of trade, your scales, your measures, and you will find this saying written on them. You will not be able to look anywhere it does not strike your eyes. None of the things with which you deal daily are too trifling to tell you this incessantly, if you are but willing to hear it; and there is not lack of such preaching for you have as many preachers as there are transactions, commodities, tools and other implements in your house and estate; and they shout this to your face, "My dear, use me toward your neighbor as you would want him to act toward you with that which is his."*

Luther believed the ministry of a barrel maker is every bit as important and valid as that of a parish minister. In no way could it be construed as inferior. In no way was the priest entitled to lord it over the worker. Who was the greatest? Both were great so long as they served their Lord.

To my mind it is the saddest feature of the contemporary Church that we have lost a vital sense of lay ministry. By and large the Church takes much too limited a view of Christian service. We eagerly recruit people necessary to maintain ourselves as an institutuion, but we do not equip you to be ministers in the world, in your daily lives within your occupations and public life. A decade ago, the National Council of Churches presented the results of its "Listening-to-Lay People Project." The report concluded:

*Lay people continue to see themselves in their expected role of servants of the institutional church. No one proposed that the church should see as its major task to encourage and enable its laypeople to function as crucial change agents in the various institutions in which they live and work. So accustomed are laypeople to turning to the church as the place where they live out their faith, that they go on separating their secular lives from their faith. They worship God in their churches, and serve the churches as best they can both in their institutions and service projects. But they do not find, nor seem to expect, much inspiration or guidance from the church at the most crucial levels of their lives — where they carry out their daily work and influence.*

This report is all too terribly true! Not long ago one of our very talented and dedicated young members was elected to the school board. She came to me to say she would have to give up a position on a church committee. She was very apologetic and seemed to feel quite guilty about it. "I want to serve the church, but I just won't have as much time for it this year," she said. I responded: "But if you serve well on the school board, you will be serving the church faithfully. You will have an opportunity to minister in a way few other people do." Then we talked for a while about what it might mean for her to minister in her new position. Even so, I could see when she left that she was reluctant to believe her new position could be considered a valid ministry. How very sad!

Luther and Calvin suggested that ministry happens

whenever a person tries to make a connection between his life and faith. If you try to analyze situations which arise at work, at home, or in the community in terms of your Christian responsibility, then you have a ministry. Ministry means leading a life of service wherever you may be.

Of course, often it is difficult to relate our faith to our life. Consider your workplace, for example. Some questions arise which can be answered quite easily, questions like: Should I cheat my partner or defraud my customers? But when your questions become more difficult, the process of relating the gospel to the world becomes more complicated. Suppose, for instance, you are a manager ordered by your company's higher-ups to implement a policy which you are sure will have adverse social impact. What do you do? Where does your loyalty lie? To your company? Or to society? What is the basis for your choice? Last year our men's study group spent some time trying to relate Christianity to very specific instances of business decisionmaking. How necessary that is, and yet how frustrating it can be when we cease to content ourselves with glib generalities and get down to hard specifics.

But while the work of lay ministry is not very easy, it is vital and necessary if the Gospel is to permeate the world. James Gilliom reminds us of a rule in the early New England churches which stated:

*If any person or persons shall be guilty of speaking against the minister — in any shape, form, or manner — or of speaking against his preaching, said person or persons shall be punished by fine, whipping, or banishment, or cutting off of ears.*

Not many congregations today would cut off the ears of a person for speaking out against a minister! Yet, as Gilliom goes on to say, there is another kind of brutality which takes place when the body of Christ has all its lay members cut off, and the clergyperson is expected or wants to do their work. It is brutal for the body of Christ because its most important members are those who spend their time in the wider world. It strangles Christian fellowship and prevents it from remaking the world.

All of us, you see, are Christ's ministers. Each of us has a role in sharing with others the Good News. Each of us has a calling, however dimly we may perceive it. "You are the light of the world," Jesus said to all of us. Rejoice, then, that the Gospel of our salvation is entrusted as much to you as to me. Claim your ministry! Remember that we share equally in an inestimable inheritance. By the devoted quality of our lives, let us give proof of this inheritance. We are, together, a royal priesthood. Royal not in that we can claim some special prerogative, but royal because we are servants, wherever we may be, of the Servant of servants.

# Out of the Barnyard

## FIFTH SUNDAY IN LENT
### John 11:1-53

*When he had said this, he cried with a loud voice, "Lazarus, come out."*
— John 11:43

Would it make any difference to the world if the churches were to shut their doors and never open them again? Many voices within and without the Church say no, it would make no difference. Soren Kierkegaard bemoaned the Church's indifference to its mission. Frustrated, he wrote a little parable which tells of a flock of geese who lived together in a handsome and secure barnyard. From time to time one of them would climb up on the barnyard fence and tell the other geese about the joys of flight and how they were created for something more than a barnyard existence. He reminded them of the adventures of their courageous ancestors who had flown across the trackless wastes. As he spoke, his hearers frequently nodded their heads in agreement. Once in a while they even flapped their wings a bit. But they never flew. The barnyard was too safe and the corn was too good.

Too often in history the Church has resembled that comfortable barnyard. This can be said, for example, of the Church in England during the eighteenth century. An urban society was emerging and there were new towns like Dickens' Coketown, "towns of machinery and tall chimneys, out of which interminable serpents of smoke trailed themselves forever and ever, and never went uncoiled.'' But the established church was slow to respond to this situation, and the urban poor grew up beyond its care. As the industrial revolution accelerated, children were made to work long hours in the new factories and had no opportunity for education or moral training. Their future was likely to consist of disease or debtors' prison, but the Church did not fly to their side.

Then, too, both the Catholic and Protestant churches of Germany in the 1930's were content by and large to lead a barnyard existence. A prominent historian writes that if the churches had opposed Hitler early on, he probably would not have come to power. Instead the churches acquiesced in Hitler's rise and even supported him at times. They rang their bells to salute Nazi victories until they were taken away to be melted down for the German war effort.

In contrast to these barnyard Christians stand Jesus' original disciples. Jesus said to them: ''You shall be my witnesses in Jerusalem and in all Judea and Samaria and to the end of the earth.'' The disciples moved far beyond their local barnyard. Their experience of the resurrection sent them forth to an unceasing ministry of mission and service that shaped the early Church. So seriously did they take Jesus' parable of the Great Judgment in Matthew 25, his imperative that they feed the hungry and clothe the naked, that we read in the Acts of the Apostles there was not a needy person among them. Their example forces the twentieth century Church to measure itself against its ancient heritage.

Many voices within and without the Church say we come up short. Recently, for example, forty-four leading citizens in Hartford, Connecticut, were polled about their perception of the Church's role in the community. Many of these leaders charged that clergy and lay people "don't really care very much about the world around them" and are "hesitant to take risks in behalf of what they feel to be morally right." They believed the religious community has "special credibility and authority to bring to public life," but they described the role of the churches in the public arena with words such as "passive, reactive, irrelevant, selfish, timid, and weak."

In a similar vein Colin Williams, who was Dean of the Yale Divinity School, has indicted the local church for its indifference to human suffering. St. Paul admonished the Philippians to have the mind of Christ, the mind of a servant people. But the local church has failed to take the shape of a servant, Williams says. It is too much a self-serving institution, located in the suburbs where it tries to forget the sorrows of the poor.

Of course there have been glorious exceptions to this pattern of indifference. In eighteenth century England, for instance, a Gloucester reformer named Robert Raikes, who believed that nobody was beyond the range of Christian compassion, flew out of the barnyard and into the wretched slums. Through his efforts the modern Sunday school was born. Then, too, in the 1930's the German theologian Dietrich Bonhoeffer was a prominent exception to the general pattern. He left his post at Union Seminary in New York to return to Germany and contend against Hitler. Eventually he was executed, but his prison writings are an enduring testament to God's power and the invincible human spirit. In our own day and land, Hubert Humphrey told a group of Protestant ministers that the 1964 Civil Rights Act could never have been passed without the support and work of the churches.

Still I think it is fair to say the contemporary Church comes up short when it is measured against its ancient heritage. Indeed, the churches which are growing the fastest these days are those which address their parishioners personal needs but do not speak to the world's larger concerns. Many people who are joining churches these days are like geese looking for good corn and a safe barnyard, and that is all they are looking for. They are not interested in participating with Christ in his ministry to the poor.

What, then, are we going to do? We could, of course, quit the Church in disillusionment as have many people. We tend to think that people will leave the Church if we deal with controversial social issues; but as Reinhold Niebuhr said once, it probably is the case that we lose more people, or more people stay away, precisely because we do not deal with the pressing issues of the day. We could stay home with these unhappy folks, but that is not a very viable alternative. That would leave the barnyard in the hands of the earthbound geese, and then the Church would be doomed indeed.

Instead let us listen to the words of our lesson this morning. They are as heartening as any we find in Scripture. They seem to say to the Church: Do not give up on yourself. Jesus had only to shout to Lazarus: "Come out"— and he did. Lazarus arose from the darkened tomb. If we will but listen for our Master's voice, so will we. So will this church. We will fly out of this barnyard and into the world where we belong.

John tells us, you see, that Jesus loved Lazarus. So, too, he loves his Church, for as a great hymn has it: "from heaven he came and sought her to be his holy bride; and with his own blood he bought her and for her life he died." Jesus loves the Church as he loved his friend, and so he calls to us just as he called to Lazarus. Our Lord is standing among the starving and humiliated of the world, and he calls to us: "Come to me. Come out of your barnyard of indifference. Lift your wings and fly. Fly to the hurting edge of the world, there to serve the poor as I have served you."

All around us, if we will but look, we will see people in need of deeds which embody the Good News. We will see the unemployed, the poorly housed, the hungry, the sick, and the troubled. God expects us to serve these people. If we are a church which claims the apostolic faith, we will reach out to them in service.

This was done with great effect, as David King relates, by the Oakland Beach Congregational Church in Warwick, Rhode Island. In 1972 Pastor Alfred Colby received a call from the nearby Institute of Mental Health, asking him to conduct a funeral service for a person who had just died there. Colby did not know the man. Commenting on his death, he said: "To my sadness I found out that no one knew this person, and I found it hard to believe that we as a Christian culture can lose people in institutions and never shed a tear."

But out of Colby's pastoral concern for this dead stranger has come a marvelous program for the living patients at the Institute. This program makes it possible for patients to leave the institution as often as possible, to work with their hands, and to socialize with people in the larger community who are volunteers from the local church. This program has become the model for a wide variety of other programs which meet the needs of the elderly, of the physically handicapped, and of low-income families. It seems the members of Oakland Beach are flying high!

We hear much these days in the mainline churches about elaborate campaigns to evangelize or recruit new members, but really it is service which will revitalize the Church. We are being told by our denominational officials that we need to work to bring in new members, but really it is only when the old members go out into the world that a church can be born again. God has given us wings, and Christ has called us to use them. It is exciting to fly, and we will find as we make our ascent that other people will be drawn naturally to our side. Consider the way Mother Teresa has captured the imagination of believer and unbeliever alike. Where local congregations become faithful servants of the poor in their midst, they, too, will capture the attention and loyalty of those who once disdained them for their indifference.

To be sure, the needs of the world seem overwhelming compared to the resources of the Church. How quick we are to see our inadequacy, to find reasons for sitting in the barnyard. If we see only our inadequacy, however, we mislead ourselves, for we need always to remember that when we are faithful, God will multiply the effect of our effort and give us the victory.

What should be our attitude? Its character is demonstrated in a little story which Professor Roland Bainton tells about Naphtali Daggett, who was President of Yale and Professor of Divinity when the American Revolution began. On July 4, 1779, the British landed a force of twenty-five hundred men at New Haven and some one-hundred students volunteered to fight a delaying action. As they were marching over West Bridge, they saw the aged Dr. Daggett "riding furiously by on his old black mare with his long fowling-piece in his hand." The students cheered him, and then they were quickly dispersed by the British. But Daggett, from under the cover of the bushes, kept on firing his fowling-piece at the redcoats until he was routed out. The British commander, seeing but one man in a black coat, exclaimed: "What are you doing there, you old fool, firing on his Majesty's troops?"

"Exercising the rights of war," replied the Congregationalist minister.

"If I let you go this time, you rascal, will you ever fire again on the troops of His Majesty."

Undaunted, Dr. Daggett replied: "Nothing is more likely." He then was marched at bayonet point some five miles through the hot sun back to New Haven.

Now Daggett seems almost a funny, pathetic figure, taking on the British force singlehandedly as he did. Sometimes, when it looks at the forces of darkness in this world, the Church must surely feel as he did, nearly overwhelmed. But I do believe that if we could muster something of Dr. Daggett's indomitable spirit, we could give those forces quite a beating. To be sure, we find in our world, as the Israelites found in ancient Canaan, "giants" whom we detest and fear. The majority report will always be: We cannot defeat them, let us turn back. But the Church needs always to take the stand of Caleb and Joshua who said: "We are well able to overcome."

We need to fly out of our comfortable barnyard with the boldness of Dr. Daggett. With Christ at our head, we need not fear the earth's hostile powers any more than the venerable divinity professor feared His Majesty's soldiers. In Eugene O'Neill's play, *Lazarus Laughed,* the resurrected Lazarus laughs at the Roman emperor Tiberius when he threatens to put him to death. Lazarus laughs because he knows no one can destroy an immortal soul. So, too, the congregation which puts on the armor of God can laugh in confidence at the powers which menace it. They cannot destroy the Church. Against the Church, Jesus said, the gates of death cannot prevail.

Reformation is the law of the Church's life. The Church needs always to be reformed in the image of its Head who poured out his life in love and service. Whenever the Church has listened to the voice of its Master and received from him the key to life, it has been emboldened to dare great things. When Martin Luther heard God's word, he was empowered to leave the monastery and to unleash a force that reshaped the

Church and the world. How many times the little Protestant movement looked as if it would be stamped out. But God fanned the tiny sparks into a veritable flame and baptized his Church with new vision and vigor.

God, I believe, has such a blessing of power in store for his Church today. We will inherit the blessing as we respond to the call of Christ who is standing among the lost and wounded. We will forfeit the blessing if we remain in our comfortable barnyard, our tomb of indifference, content merely to flap our wings a little bit from time to time. Pray, then, that the Church may be graced with the ear of faith, with the ear of Lazarus, to hear its Master calling. Our Lord is calling to us even now as he did once to his beloved Lazarus. As he did once to his dear friend, he is shouting now to his beloved but entombed Church: "Come out!"

And live.

# The Grace of Disillusionment

## SUNDAY OF THE PASSION
### Matthew 26:1-27:66

*And he went out and wept bitterly.*

— Matthew 26:75b

In his famous autobiography, Henry Adams wrote of his chronic irritability. He thought it was the result of knowing too much about his neighbors and thinking too much of himself. We have in Luke's parable of the Pharisee and the publican a man who, like the early Henry Adams, combines a low opinion of his neighbors with a high estimate of his own qualities. The Pharisee's prayer in chapter eighteen is taken from life, for a similar prayer comes to us in the Talmud in the first century A.D.:

> *I thank thee, O Lord, my God, that thou has given me my lot with those who sit in the seat of learning, and not with those who sit at the street corner; for I am early to work, and they are early to work; I am early to work on the words of the Torah, and they are early to work on things of no moment. I weary myself, and they weary themselves; I weary myself and profit thereby, while they weary themselves to no profit. I run and they run; I run towards the life of the Age to come, and they run towards the pit of destruction.*

Here, then, from the Pharisee, is a prayer of thanksgiving: "God, I thank thee that I am not like other men."

The publican, on the other hand, runs toward the pit of destruction, or so the Pharisee supposes. Customs collectors had many ways to cheat the public and made a lot of money doing it. Respectable people despised them. No wonder the man does not dare to lift his eye to heaven. He is bitterly aware of his distance from God and can only beat his breast in contrition. He and his family are in a hopeless situation. To repent, he will need not only to quit his way of life, but also to restore his dishonest gains with an added fifth in damages. He does not even know all those with whom he has had dealings! Even his prayer strikes a note of hopelessness. He cannot fathom that God's mercy might run so deep as to embrace his own wretched need.

The parable's ending must have stunned its hearers. Luke says they were people who trusted in themselves that they were righteous and despised others. Jesus says to them: "I tell you, this man, this miserable tax collector, went down to his house justified rather than the other; for everyone who exalts himself will be humbled, but he who humbles himself will be exalted."

This pronouncement seems almost an insult to our sense of propriety. The Pharisee has committed no fault and through his fasting and tithing has done more by way of religious observance than the law requires. The publican, on the other hand, while he is apologetic, has done nothing to repay the aggrieved parties. But Jesus does not respond to our questions. He says only that this is God's decision. This, simply, is the way God is.

Of course we have a clue as to what Jesus has in mind. The publican's prayer appropriates the opening words of Psalm 51: "Have mercy on me, O God." As Joachim Jeremias observes, we find in that same psalm a verse which reads: "The sacrifice acceptable to God is a broken spirit; a broken and contrite heart, O God, thou wilt not despise." Here, Jesus suggests, is what God is like. God greets the hopeless sinner, but he rejects the self-confident and the self-righteous. As Pascal wrote: There are only two kinds of men: the righteous who believe themselves sinners, and the rest, sinners who believe themselves righteous."

I speak at some length of Luke's famous parable because in our lesson from Matthew, we witness what might be called the "de-Phariseeification" of Peter. Like the Pharisee, Peter believed his faith was impeccable. He was so sure of himself that he could say in Jerusalem he was willing to die with Jesus. Of course when the hour of testing came, he failed miserably, and the layers of his pride were peeled off like onion skins until nothing remained. Then "he went out and wept bitterly."

This was a great thing for Peter, however. Profound Christian living always begins in tears of repentance. Karl Menninger writes that a suffering conscience can bring about an experience of repentance which leads to a higher level of life. This certainly was true for Peter. Peter's disillusionment with himself in the hour of crisis demolished all his vain pretensions. Then, like the publican, he could only cry out with agonized sincerity: Have mercy on me, a sinner. In humility he could begin to recognize his utter dependence upon God. His eyes were opened to see the God whose grace and judgment had been molding him. Peter's shame was an opportunity for God to begin in him a ministry that would be fruitful as was that of Jesus himself. Not until this point could Peter really say he belonged to the Lord.

What of you and me? Is ours the mind of the Pharisee or the publican? In his story, "Goodbye, My Brother," John Cheever gives us a portrait of a modern day Pharisee. Lawrence Pommeroy is an unhappy

Albany lawyer who is reunioning with his family at their summer place on the shore of a Massachusetts island. They are an old New England family, descended from a Puritan minister, but by and large they have managed to slough off the ancient habits of guilt, self-denial, taciturnity, and penitence. By stern standards, they are somewhat dissolute, fond of drinking, gambling over backgammon, and partying. But not Lawrence. His Puritan inheritance remains intact. He is not a religious man, but he is a man of principle. He devotes his time to lecturing his family about their frailties. He is a man who trusts totally in his own righteousness and so, quite inevitably, despises other people.

It is necessary, given his cast of mind, that Lawrence Pommeroy will forever quit his family at the end of the story. "I have important things to do," he says as he issues his last good-bye. Separation is always the price of self-righteousness. The Pharisee, Luke writes, stood by himself. He kept himself aloof from the other worshipers. He was, to borrow Augustine's adjective, "incurved," turned in on himself, preoccupied by his own merit. His self-righteousness could issue only in contempt for those he supposed to be running toward the pit of destruction. A soul closed to God is closed as well to brothers and sisters. So Pharisees, be they ancient or modern, are left in a hell of their own making. In hell, writes Lewis Mumford, there is no community. It is not possible.

Lawrence Pommeroy is a man of our time, disillusioned by every encounter, relationship, and arrangement. He deserves something better, he believes, but never finding it, he lives in despair. "Come out of this gloominess, come out of it!" his brother beseeches him. But he cannot. He is too aware of his own goodness and too sure of other people's wrong. Like the early Henry Adams, he knows too much about his neighbors and thinks too much of himself.

Most of us, I think, have something of the Pharisee in us, and so it is that we live in a "good-bye" world. The Church, for example, does not live up to our expectations. Robert Frost said he had a lover's quarrel with the world. I think many of us have a lover's quarrel with the Church. The Church seems more human than divine. It does not live up to our hopes. In the Gospel we have a healing word for a war-racked world, but then we find we have not learned even to handle conflict in our own small circle. That is disillusioning. For some it is so disillusioning that the lover's quarrel becomes a mean-spirited thing. They quit the Church, embittered. "We are not like those other people," they think to themselves. "We would never do such terrible things." Perhaps they look for another church home, one where human frailty will not be so much in evidence and where the other people will be up to their own exacting standards of righteousness.

Then, too, our nation is saying its good-byes. In the 1960's we committed ourselves through national legislation to the creation of a fairer society, to the abolition of poverty and racism. Our programs accomplished much, but they did not prove to be the quick and complete fix for which we hoped. So now, wearied and discouraged, we permit our economy's focus to shift away from the creative and more just society to one which utilizes its resources to build nuclear weapons at the risk of holocaust. As surely as Lawrence Pommeroy, we are saying our "good-byes" to our churches and to our highest ideals.

What can you do with a man like Lawrence Pommeroy? his brother asks. What can you do about the Lawrence Pommeroys of the world? What can we do about the Lawrence Pommeroy, the Pharisee, in each of us breeds disillusionment and gloom? The first step, Jesus says, is to see ourselves for what we really are. "Why do you see the speck that is in your brother's eye, but do not notice the log that is in your own eye?'' he says. He suggests to us that we must permit the process of disillusionment to carry full-circle, to include not just the rest of the world but ourselves as well. We are like the Pharisee in the temple, or like Peter before Jesus' arrest. We thank God we are not like other men and women. We do not understand that we are indeed like others! We may not be robbers or cheats, but we are incurved, more preoccupied by our own plans and concerns than with God's purposes. You know, a man once approached Jesus with the words, ''Good teacher,'' and Jesus rebuked him. ''Why do you call me good?'' he demanded. ''Only the Father who is in heaven is good.'' ''If we say we have no sin,'' writes St. John, ''we deceive ourselves.''

This is who we are, and until we recognize our need of God's mercy, until we cease to speak of ''those'' sinners and speak instead of ''us'' sinners, well then we are in the position of the Pharisee. A prospective church member once told a deacon that he would not be joining the church because he had discovered it was full of hypocrites. ''That's all right,'' the deacon responded. ''There's always room for one more.'' Pogo observed: ''We have met the enemy, and he is us.'' Until we grasp this truth, that we are part of the common human denominator, we will stand aloof from the world. For as long as we know too much of our neighbors and think too much of ourselves, we are like those islanders whom Herman Melville described as Isolatoes. ''Isolatoes,'' he called them, ''not acknowledging the common continent of men, but each Isolato living in a separate continent of his own.'' Only when we are unburdened of our self-righteousness, of our vain pretensions, and begin to appreciate our shared identity, only then will be become full partners in this human enterprise.

More than anyone who has walked on this earth, Jesus of Nazareth was entitled to be disappointed and disillusioned by life. He provided his disciples with many examples of sacrificial service, but he found them arguing about their rank. Of all the people entitled to walk away in anger, Jesus certainly possessed first claim. But instead, the Gospel says, out of his love for the world, he endured the agony of the cross. If anyone were ever to have been justified in declaring: "I thank thee, God, that I am not like other men" — it would have been this same Jesus whom the Gospels say was without sin. But he said such a prayer was the word of a soul cut off from God, the mind of one who does not understand that he depends for life upon God. Can we not see how Isaac Watts could consider Jesus' life and write: "I survey the wondrous cross and pour contempt on all my pride."

This morning we come to our Lord's house as publicans, with a sense of our unworthiness, leaving behind the Pharisee's pretence. We come as brothers and sisters who share the full range of human sinfulness, but we know, too, of God's fathomless mercy which covers our heads. We come unhappy with others in our midst, perhaps, but we do not come to say good-bye to them, for that would leave us each to his own continent. We are, all of us, children of God, implicated in the one destiny of the one human family. With publicans of every time, we come here looking for God to "pierce the gloom of our sin and grief," hoping to feel on our faces the warmth of a rising sun. "Lord, have mercy," is our common prayer. And the Author of our salvation promises it will be as we ask.

# Loving Unconditionally

## MAUNDY THURSDAY
### John 13:1-17, 34

*"A new commandment I give to you, that you love one another . . ."*

The love which Christians show for one another has always been a compelling, even unanswerable argument for the truth of our faith. Jesus said: "By this all men will know that you are my disciples, if you have love for one another." So well did the early Christians follow Jesus' prescription that it was said of them: "See how they love each other." St. John Chrysostom, who was made Bishop of Constantinople in A.D. 398, remarked: "If we Christians lived as we should, non-believers would be more astonished at our lives than at miracles."

By the same token, the prejudice and intolerance exhibited by some Christians often calls into question the truth of our faith. When Gandhi was asked why he never became a Christian, he replied: "Because I have known too many Christians." The philosopher John Dewey, who so profoundly influenced the course of American public education, learned his Christianity at the hands of petty, small-minded people in his hometown. When he left his town, he left his religion behind as well.

It is easy to make the point that religious people can be unattractive and even quite dangerous, that at times they reflect more hostility than love. Through the centuries, for example, there have been Christian theologies which say it is better for a person to be dead than to live outside the Church. St. Augustine, the fifth century churchman to whom our civilization owes so much, was a great exponent of love. But he also advocated what he called "righteous persecution." He declared that people who had strayed from correct belief should be recalled lest they be condemned forever to the darkness. So he said of those outside the Church: "Compel them to come in." The power of the Roman state, which by that time was officially Christian, was used to coerce people into confessing the creeds.

Then, too, Thomas Aquinas advocated the killing of sinners. The great medieval theologian quoted Exodus 22:18 which says it is well to remove one member for the good of the whole body. He said: "If a man be dangerous and infectious to the community, on account of some sin, it is praiseworthy and advantageous that he be killed in order to safeguard the common good." This was the dominant attitude of much of medieval Christendom.

Nor were our own Puritan ancestors renowned for loving people whose views were contrary to their own. They scourged the Baptists and drove them to Rhode Island which they called the "sewer" of New England. My own ancestor was forced to move with his congregation to New Hampshire because he opposed government-enforced religious observances in the Bay Colony; yet even he despised the Quakers. Someone said once he would rather face a platoon of United States Marines than face one Puritan who was convinced he was on a mission from God and could do no wrong. St. Paul wrote that even the justified remain sinners and so need to have a certain modesty about their beliefs. Strong conviction in itself is not admirable. It needs to be tempered with humility.

With this in mind, one can begin to appreciate why

the Moral Majority arouses fear in many of our hearts — not because we are part of an immoral minority or unconcerned about what is happening in this country, but because over 1,500 years of history reveal what can happen when a group of people, convinced of its rightness to the point of self-righteousness, tries to use the power of the state to coerce other people into sharing its particular religious vision.

Herman Melville wrote:

> . . . when a man's religion becomes really frantic; when it is a positive torment to him; and, in time, makes this earth of ours an uncomfortable inn to lodge in; then I think it is high time to take that individual aside and argue the point with him.

Today, with the rise of the religious right and with the rise of anti-Semitism in some parts of our land, it seems "high time" to argue the case for religious tolerance — tolerance which is grounded not in indifference but in the love of Christ.

What is confusing is that in Scripture we seem at first to have prescriptions both for loving our opponents and for practicing "righteous persecution." Alongside Jesus' admonition for us to love even our enemies, we can put several other passages which seem to suggest a drastically different attitude. In his Pentecost sermon, for example, Peter says of Jesus: "And there is salvation in no one else, for there is no other name under heaven given among men by which we must be saved." According to the Gospel of John, Jesus claimed: "I am the way, the truth, and the life. No one comes unto the Father but by me." The risen Christ of Matthew's Gospel declares: "All power in both heaven and earth has been given to me." Paul in his letter to Philippi says that all heavenly and earthly powers must bow the knee before Christ. These passages do seem to suggest that the road to salvation is narrow indeed. One can begin to see how St. Augustine could say of the unbeliever: Compel him to come into the Church.

How do we make sense of this apparent conflict? Let us be quick to affirm that Jesus Christ is the way, the truth and the life. But then let us go on to ask if we are entirely clear in what his way consists. Let us be quick to affirm that Christ now reigns over the universe, that he is, as Scripture puts it, seated at the right hand of God. But let us go on to ask if we know what it means to participate in his power and to bear his authority. For in answering these questions, we shall discover that we have in fact a prescription not for righteous persecution, but only for love.

Scripture reveals the pattern of Jesus' life to be entirely consistent. Never did Jesus carry out his will through coercion or domination. He always used persuasion. He understood that loyalty cannot be coerced; it must be earned. He accomplished his work, not through the exercise of power or by brow-beating, but through his word and by his humble deeds of love. "The greatest among you must be your servant," he told his disciples. To make his point, he washed the feet of his disciples, a task undertaken ordinarily by only the most menial servants. That was Jesus' way, and his deeds were his authority. It was in this way that he won people to his cause. Jesus loved people unconditionally. He did not insist that those whom he helped conform to his own theology. His behavior was gracious, not only to the inhabitants of the house of Israel, but to the Samaritan woman and to the Roman official. He knew that people would come to love and serve God only if first they were shown what God is like. "Let your light so shine . . ." he said.

Now it is true to say that the way of Jesus is narrow; but it is the narrow path of unswerving, unstinting, unbounded compassion. It is the way of a love which, in

Paul's words, is "patient and kind, not jealous or boastful, not arrogant or rude, not insistent on its own way, not irritable or resentful." That is the way of Jesus, and if we in the Christian churches really believe that Jesus is the only way to God, if we want really to make his way our way, then we will spend less time scourging our theological opponents and more time looking for opportunities to serve a world which groans in travail. We will do this not because beliefs are unimportant, but we will do this because the first claim God makes on us is to love each other, not to get our theologies right.

Please do not misunderstand me here. I am not advocating the kind of attitude Chesterton had in mind when he wrote that tolerance is the virtue of a people who do not believe in anything. That is a passive kind of tolerance and is grounded in uncaring ignorance. It is reflected, for example, in the often heard statement that Christians should tolerate other religions because they are all the same anyway. This is true in part because all major religions do afrirm human dignity. In a world beset by dehumanizing forces, this is no small thing. But there are also some significant differences among faiths. Christians, for instance, believe that religion is not so much people seeking God as God seeking people. The Divine Shepherd seeks out the lost sheep. Salvation is only of the Lord. Buddhists, on the other hand, believe that religion is people reaching toward God and working their own way up the ladder of salvation, seeking Nirvana. These are not mere academic differences! Our understanding of God shapes our perception of who we are. How we understand human nature has implications for our styles of morality and politics. Christians are called to be tolerant of other religions and of Christians who hold to different doctrines — not because they are all the same anyway, but because the primary claim God makes on us is not to get our theologies right, but to love each other, unconditionally.

St. Paul understood this perfectly. No one was more argumentative than he. He seems to have enjoyed a good theological row. No one had more definite ideas about what theological formulations were true to God's work in Christ, and what theology was misleading. His letter to Rome is a theological argument, the most precious in the Church's possession, and one which sparked the great work of Augustine, Luther, Wesley, and Barth. In Romans Paul does not shirk from his case or pull any punches. But it is imperative to note the context in which he sets his case. He does not begin with argument. Where does he begin? He begins by expressing his love for the Christians gathered in Rome who are reading his words. "First, I thank my God through Jesus Christ for all of you," he writes. "For God is my witness, whom I serve with my spirit in the gospel of his son, that without ceasing I mention you always in my prayers." Only then does Paul begin to make his case. He sets it in the context of Christian love which is the essential, enduring bond among Christian people. Where that bond is established, people have nothing to fear from their disagreements.

So we have in the gospel of Jesus Christ and in the words of the gospel's greatest exponent, a formula for a love which can "bear all things," even the presence about us of people with whom we vigorously disagree. God loves everyone, we are told, whether they love him or not. Because God loves them, so must we. "We love," John writes, "because God first loved us." There is no precedent in the Christian gospel for Augustine's policy of "righteous persecution" or for any similar, subsequent policy or attitude. Love does not insist on its own way.

Often I am reminded that in this congregation we have very different theologies. We have different ideas about the mission of the Church, about the character of God, and the interpretation of Scripture. Now we can and must differ with each other as our consciences dictate. But I believe that in the way of Christ we find a unity which is larger than our disunities. The way of Christ is the way of love, and it is the power to bind all of us together. Doctrine is important, and I believe that some theological expressions are truer to the great insights of the gospel than are others. But I am also convinced that there is nothing to be gained by theological debate unless it is approached in the spirit of love, in the spirit of Jesus as he washed the feet of his disciples, or in the way of Paul in his letter to the Romans. For only when we love one another, do we become willing to put ourselves in another's shoes. Only then, when we try to see the world as another sees it, do we risk having our own ideas changed. And changed and enlarged our ideas must surely be, for as the Pilgrim's pastor, John Robinson, said: "It is too great arrogancy for any man to think that he has sounded the word of God to the bottom." Then, as our ideas change and enlarge, I believe we will discover a way to knit together the common threads of our competing theologies and so upbuild the Church.

Brethren, let us forever remember the words of Paul and take them as our rule: "Faith, hope, love abide, these three, but the greatest of these is love." Let us remember that love itself, as revealed by God's only son, is patient and kind, never arrogant or rude.

# Victim or Visionary

## GOOD FRIDAY
## John 18:1-19:42

*And again another scripture says, "They shall look upon him whom they have pierced."*

— John 19:37

On the cross, our Lord must have looked at the faces of his executioners and experienced the sharp frustration which comes from being subject to principalities and powers beyond one's capacity to shape or control. For a time, he must have felt like a helpless victim of cruel, cosmic circumstance. You and I, then, should not have too much trouble empathizing with the crucified Jesus. We, too, are beset by forces which seem beyond our capacity to mold or influence. Consider, for example, the Tylenol poisonings and their impact upon our national consciousness; how they underscored our frightening vulnerability. In our society, it seems, there is no end to the process of creating victims.

Psychiatrists, for instance, have learned that many children are psychological victims of the nuclear arms race. Children are experiencing acute mental distress as they contemplate the very real possibility they will not grow up. They see themselves as victims of an adult world which is unable to settle disputes in an intelligent way. Many adults feel much the same of course. We see ourselves as victims of a system of international security which produces more stress, anxiety, and fear than it does protection.

But the prospect of nuclear war is only one cause of victimization. Our limping economy is producing millions of victims. People in this congregation who have given their companies years of loyal and competent service now find themselves out of work. Furthermore, even when times are good, the business world sometimes creates victims. I know from personal experience that many people believe their religious and moral beliefs are victimized by corporate pressures. They find it difficult to integrate their faith and their work in day-to-day corporate decisionmaking. Their personal ethics are of the highest order, but they find it hard to discern and implement ethical imperatives at work. *The New Yorker* magazine captured this distinction in a cartoon. A husband returns home, briefcase in hand, very late at night. His wife greets him in her bathrobe and with a stern expression. He says to her: "Edna, how could you think for a moment that I'd be capable of any shenanigans, except at the corporate level!" We smile at that, but these corporate shenanigans can exact their personal toll. They can create their victims.

My debating partner in college was a boy named Lee Black. His father was Eli Black, a rabbi who had left the synagogue for the business world. He was a savvy corporate strategist and became chairman of United Brands. United Brands was a highly successful company which also enjoyed a reputation for being one of the most socially conscious corporations in this hemisphere. But United Brands had to compete in Latin America, and the time came, when, in order to compete, it had to make an illegal payment to an official of the Honduran government. It was something other companies were doing, but Eli Black was too sensitive to live with this procedure, and it claimed his life. With agonized conscience, he jumped to his death from the forty-fourth floor of the Pan Am building in Manhattan.

Then, too, some of us have been participating recently in a series of workshops on family life. We have been learning about victimization in marriage and in the family: How a married couple's relationship can be the victim of the frenzied pressures associated with raising children; how a young person's character can be the victim of parents who refuse to discipline him; how a young person's character can be the victim of parents who refuse to give him room to grow and develop. So it is that I say there seems no end to the process of creating victims. The affairs of this world, of our work and of our family life, all cast us at times in the role of victim.

However, here is a question for you. It is a question for everyone who feels helpless. Are you only a victim? Is that all you can say about yourself? That you are a victim of your world? Or can you say something more for yourself?

There are many voices which say we must be content to be victims. It seems to me that Freud, who powerfully shaped the modern consciousness, said just that. He said essentially that people are sick animals, dominated by untamed passions, victims of irrational instincts. There are many voices which echo his understanding and which prophesy our collective doom. I do not feel I need to catalogue these for you, for when you turn this afternoon to your paper, I am confident you will see them dutifully and reverently quoted.

Instead, on this day, on this darkest of days, I want to ask you to listen to a different voice. To listen to the Gospel of Jesus Christ. For you see Christ's gospel rejects the prevailing view that we are predestined to be victims; that we must, as did the sailors in Shakespeare's *Tempest,* despair because all is almost lost. This Christian voice makes us restless and dissatisfied with playing the role of victim, with the life that merely creeps. It speaks to us instead of the glorious possibilities of the soul. It does this without glossing over the unhappy portion of our lives. Do not think for a moment that there is anything sentimental or naive or pollyanna about the gospel. If there were, I could not stand here Sunday after Sunday and preach to you, for by now I have seen too much of life's dark underbelly. I have been too many times to the grave, to the hospital, to the unhappy home and to the slum. I know that life can be mean, and I think that Christianity is nothing if it is not realistic about this.

But always it is. Always our faith is frank and open-eyed. So it is that in Chapter 8 of Romans, Paul speaks of the sufferings of the present time, the slavery to decay, and the groans and agonies. He catalogues our afflictions: tribulation, distress, persecution, famine, nakedness, peril, sword, death and principalities. Let's admit it, he says. Life is like this.

But while Paul acknowledges this, he does not sit down and indulge in the cheap luxury of self-pity, nor does he wallow in the slough of despair. He does not try to gloss over the grim elements of life, but he does know something that many modern minds do not. He knows that these unhappy elements are but one part of the human story. He knows there is another part of this story — and that is the reality of God. So he says: "What, then, shall we say to these things: peril, sword, death, and the others?" And he rejoins: "If God be for us, who can be against us." Yes, life can be mean, Paul says, but let us remember also that with the worst there is the best. Always there is God; and of his love we have had rich experience. In every encounter with adversity, there is God himself: the God who makes himself known in the life and most especially in the death of the victimized lamb, Jesus Christ.

Yes, you heard me correctly. I said that God makes himself known most especially in the death of his Son.

That seems at first a strange thing to say because Christians sometimes speak of this as the day when the Father abandoned the Son. Indeed some people consider the murder of the noble Galilean to be a proof there is no God at all. Our twentieth century cry that God is dead was anticipated before Jesus' birth by a character in Euripides, who, seeing there was no moral order in human affairs, argued there can be no God:

> Doth someone say that there be gods above? There are not; no there are not. Let no fool, led by the old false fable, thus deceive you. Look at the facts themselves.

The fact of the crucifixion seems at first to be proof that "truth is on the scaffold and wrong is on the throne." As Paul says, however, the cross destroys the "wisdom of the wise." I believe that we see on this day not some momentary lapse in God's love, but rather its supreme revelation.

When the soldier lanced Jesus' side, you see, he meant to demonstrate that he was dead. By doing that, John writes, he fulfilled the Scripture from Zechariah 12 which says: "They shall look on him whom they have pierced." As Raymond Brown observes, what is interesting is that just before this verse we read these words of Yahweh: "I shall pour out on the house of David and the inhabitants of Jerusalem a spirit of compassion." Jesus' wounding, then, is actually the beginning of life. From Jesus' side flows that living water which is the source of life. On the cross Jesus fulfills his own words: "And just as Moses lifted up the serpent in the desert, so must the Son of Man be lifted up, that everyone who believes may have eternal life in him." So it is that the cross becomes a symbol of life and love. Only the cross is powerful enough to win the souls of men and women to the cause of God. Isaac

Watts surveyed the "wondrous cross" and wrote:

*Were the whole realm of nature mine,*
*That were a present far too small;*
*Love so amazing, so divine,*
*Demands my soul, my life, my all.*

Only by love "so amazing" could God win our hearts and minds.

What I am saying here about the necessity and power of the cross was illustrated beautifully some years ago in the movie called "The Pawnbroker." The protagonist is an immigrant named Sol Nazerman who is a pawn merchant in a little shop in Harlem. Having lost his wife and children in a Nazi deathcamp, he is determined never to be injured again, and he has become indifferent to the suffering which every day he witnesses. Pathethic people come to his shop: a teenage drug addict needing money for a fix and a father who has to sell a pair of bronzed baby shoes after the child dies. But Nazerman is callous and uncaring. His compassion is the victim of his own miserable history.

The climax occurs when his Puerto Rican assistant, a boy named Jesus Ortiz, joins a gang of hoodlums. The gang comes to the shop to rob the old man. Unexpectedly, one of the boys draws a gun and starts to shoot him. Jesus, though, throws himself on the gun and is killed. The other boys run off, leaving the pawnbroker to hold the head of the dying Jesus. Then, as one critic put it, the man's "humanity returns in a torrent." With his eyes blinded by tears, he goes back into the shop, and we see what he is going to do. There is a paperspike before him. The old man places his hand over the spike and forces it down. Finally, with the hand bleeding, he goes away to rejoin the world in its groaning — to be not a victim but, like Jesus Ortiz, an instrument of redemption.

It has been said that Jane Austen despised the greater number of her characters. George Eliot, on the other hand, suffered with each of hers. God is like George Eliot. He suffers with his characters. He suffers with you and me! If God himself has suffered, then there is meaning for our suffering.

W.H. Auden has noted that for the ancient Greeks of Homer's day:

> *Life is unbearably sad because it never trans-cends the immediate moment; one is happy, one is unhappy, one wins, one loses, finally one dies. That is all. Joy and suffering are simply what one feels at the moment; they have no meaning beyond that; they pass away as they came; they point in no direction; they change nothing* (quoted in *The Portable Greek Reader.*)

But Christ's suffering has changed something. It has changed us. His amazing love strikes us in our pride and emboldens us to take up our own cross. No longer are we victims. Now we are agents of God's redemptive mission. As Auden reminds us in "Memorial":

> *Our grief is not Greek: As we bury our dead*
> *We know without knowing there is reason for*
>     *what we bear,*
> *That our hurt is not a desertion, that we are to*
>     *pity*
> *Neither ourselves nor our city;*
> *. . . We are not to despair.*

No, we are not to despair because life is ever lord over death. This is the ultimate reality of our world. Not wishful thinking, mind you, but fact. One of the most eloquent testimonies to this fact I know comes from Sadako Kurihara in a little booklet prepared by our

Board for World Ministries. From her experience in
Hiroshima on August 6, 1945, she wrote this poem:

*It was night in the basement of a destroyed
    building.*
*The wounded from the atomic bombing*
*Crowded the dark room*
*Without even the light of one candle.*
*The smell of new blood and of dead bodies
    accompanied*
*The panting and groaning.*

*From the midst of the weary came*
*A voice filled with wonder:*
*"A baby is coming!"*
*In this basement, like the pits of hell,*
*At this very moment a young woman was
    beginning labor.*

*What would be done?*
*In this darkness without a single match?*

*They were anxious, forgetting their own pain.*
*"I'll help. I'm a midwife," said*
*A woman, herself gravely wounded.*
*Only a moment before she too had been
groaning.*
*In this way, in the very depths of fathomless hell,*
*A new life was born.*
*But the midwife, unable to endure until dawn,*
*Died covered with her own blood.*

*Let's give them birth.*
*Let's give them life.*
*Even if it means giving up our own.*

What about you? Are you merely a victim, or are

you something more than that? Are you a visionary? Are you a visionary like that Japanese midwife who saw life in the midst of terrible death? Are you a visionary like St. John, who even amidst the cruelty of Roman repression, even in lonely exile, saw the holy city, new Jerusalem, coming down out of heaven from God, resplendent? As you ponder the starkness of the cross, can you hear as well a voice from heaven saying: "Behold the dwelling of God is with men. He will dwell with them, and they shall be his people, and God himself will be with them." How good are your eyes? Are they encrusted with the dogmatic pessimism of this world? Or can they see the light shining in the darkness? Are you a victim? Or are you like St. John on Patmos, invincibly confident even in the darkness?

Thomas Aquinas said once that "our foes press on from every side." Today they press on in the worlds of politics, work, and family life. But we need not be their victims. As you read your afternoon paper with its terrible recitals, ponder, too, what God has done in Christ; remember that nothing is impossible to people of faith and conviction. We need only to take the whole armor of God, the helmet of salvation, and the sword of the spirit. Armed like this against our foes, we shall, in the words of Ephesians, be able to withstand in the evil day and, having done it all, to stand.